The NFL's Greatest Teams

CHICAGO BEARS

Big Buddy Books

An Imprint of Abdo Publishing
www.abdopublishing.com

Marcia Zappa

www.abdopublishing.com

Published by Abdo Publishing, a division of ABDO, PO Box 398166, Minneapolis, Minnesota 55439.
Copyright © 2015 by Abdo Consulting Group, Inc. International copyrights reserved in all countries. No part
of this book may be reproduced in any form without written permission from the publisher. Big Buddy Books™
is a trademark and logo of Abdo Publishing.

Printed in the United States of America, North Mankato, Minnesota.
042014
092014

Cover Photo: ASSOCIATED PRESS.
Interior Photos: ASSOCIATED PRESS (pp. 5, 7, 9, 11, 13, 14, 17, 18, 19, 20, 21, 25, 27, 28, 29); Danita
    Delimont (p. 23); TOM DIPACE (p. 21); NFL (p. 13).

Coordinating Series Editor: Rochelle Baltzer
Contributing Editors: Bridget O'Brien, Sarah Tieck
Graphic Design: Michelle Labatt

Library of Congress Cataloging-in-Publication Data

Zappa, Marcia, 1985-
  Chicago Bears / Marcia Zappa.
      pages cm. -- (The NFL's greatest teams)
  ISBN 978-1-62403-359-9
1. Chicago Bears (Football team)--History--Juvenile literature. I. Title.
  GV956.C5Z36 2015
  796.332'640977311--dc23
                      2013047664

Contents

A Winning Team

Time Out

Twenty-seven Bears are in the Pro Football Hall of Fame. That is more than any other team!

The Chicago Bears are a football team from Chicago, Illinois. They were one of the first teams in the National Football League (NFL).

The Bears have had good seasons and bad. But time and again, they've proven themselves. Let's see what makes the Bears one of the NFL's greatest teams.

Navy blue, orange, and white are the team's colors.

League Play

The NFL got its start in 1920. Its teams have changed over the years. Today, there are 32 teams. They make up two conferences and eight divisions.

The Bears play in the North Division of the National Football Conference (NFC). This division also includes the Detroit Lions, the Green Bay Packers, and the Minnesota Vikings.

Team Standings

The NFC and the American Football Conference (AFC) make up the NFL. Each conference has a north, south, east, and west division.

The Packers are a major rival of the Bears. Fans enjoy watching the teams face off!

Kicking Off

The Bears started out in 1920 in Decatur, Illinois. The team was founded by A.E. Staley. At first, they were called the Decatur Staleys. George Halas was the first coach. He also played on the team.

In 1921, Halas became the team owner. He moved the Staleys to Chicago. There, the team won its first **championship**! The next year, Halas changed the team's name to the Chicago Bears.

Staley (*left*) owned a starch factory. Halas (*right*) worked there as a young man.

When the Staleys moved to Chicago, they played at Wrigley Field.

OFFICIAL PROGRAM 1928

CHICAGO BEARS FOOTBALL CLUB Inc.

PRICE 10 CENTS

Wrigley Field

Highlight Reel

The Bears were the NFL **champions** in 1932, 1933, 1940, 1941, 1943, and 1946. But then, things went downhill.

In 1963, the Bears came back as NFL champions. In 1965, the team **drafted** Dick Butkus and Gale Sayers. Butkus and Sayers became star players. Still, the team didn't make the play-offs during their **careers**.

Win or Go Home

NFL teams play 16 regular season games each year. The teams with the best records are part of the play-off games. Play-off winners move on to the conference championship. Then, conference winners face off in the Super Bowl!

The first NFL Championship Game was held in 1933. Before this, the league champion was the team with the best record.

In 1975, the Bears **drafted** Walter Payton. In 1982, Jim McMahon and coach Mike Ditka joined the team. They helped make the Bears powerful.

In 1985, the Bears only lost one game during the regular season. They went on to play in their first Super Bowl in 1986. There, the Bears beat the New England Patriots 46–10.

The Bears struggled in the 1990s and early 2000s. In 2007, they played in their second Super Bowl. This time, they lost to the Indianapolis Colts 29–17.

The Bears were known for their powerful defense players in 1985.

In 1985, the Bears sang a rap song about going to the Super Bowl. It was called "The Super Bowl Shuffle."

Halftime! Stat Break

Team Records

RUSHING YARDS
Career: Walter Payton, 16,726 yards (1975–1987)
Single Season: Walter Payton, 1,852 yards (1977)

PASSING YARDS
Career: Jay Cutler, 14,913 yards and gaining (2009–)
Single Season: Erik Kramer, 3,838 yards (1995)

RECEPTIONS
Career: Walter Payton, 492 receptions (1975–1987)
Single Season: Brandon Marshall, 118 receptions (2012)

ALL-TIME LEADING SCORER
Kevin Butler, 1,116 points (1985–1995)

Famous Coaches

George Halas (1920–1929, 1933–1942, 1946–1955, 1958–1967)
Mike Ditka (1982–1992)

Championships

EARLY CHAMPIONSHIP WINS:
1921, 1932, 1933, 1940, 1941, 1943, 1946, 1963

SUPER BOWL APPEARANCES:
1986, 2007

SUPER BOWL WINS:
1986

Pro Football Hall of Famers & Their Years with the Bears

Doug Atkins, Defensive End (1955–1966)

George Blanda, Quarterback/Kicker (1949, 1950–1958)

Dick Butkus, Middle Linebacker (1965–1973)

George Connor, Tackle/Linebacker (1948–1955)

Richard Dent, Defensive End (1983–1993, 1995)

Mike Ditka, Tight End (1961–1966)

John "Paddy" Driscoll, Quarterback (1920, 1926–1929)

Jim Finks, Administrator (1974–1982)

Dan Fortmann, Guard (1936–1943)

Bill George, Linebacker (1952–1965)

Harold "Red" Grange, Halfback (1925, 1929–1934)

George Halas, Founder/Owner/Coach (1920–1983)

Dan Hampton, Defensive Tackle/Defensive End (1979–1990)

Ed Healey, Tackle (1922–1927)

Bill Hewitt, End (1932–1936)

Stan Jones, Guard/Defensive Tackle (1954–1965)

Sid Luckman, Quarterback (1939–1950)

William Roy "Link" Lyman, Tackle (1926–1928, 1930–1931, 1933–1934)

George McAfee, Halfback (1940–1941, 1945–1950)

George Musso, Tackle/Guard (1933–1944)

Bronko Nagurski, Fullback (1930–1937, 1943)

Walter Payton, Running Back (1975–1987)

Gale Sayers, Halfback (1965–1971)

Mike Singletary, Linebacker (1981–1992)

Joe Stydahar, Tackle (1936–1942, 1945–46)

George Trafton, Center (1920–1921, 1923–1932)

Clyde "Bulldog" Turner, Center/Linebacker (1940–1952)

Fan Fun

STADIUM: Soldier Field
LOCATION: Chicago, Illinois
MASCOT: Staley Da Bear

NICKNAMES: The Monsters of the Midway, Da Bears
TEAM SONG: "Bear Down, Chicago Bears"

Coaches' Corner

George Halas was a player and coach for the Bears. Later, he was the owner. He was with the team from their beginning until his death in 1983. This earned him the nickname "Papa Bear." When he stopped coaching after the 1967 season, he had 324 wins!

Mike Ditka played for the Bears in the 1960s. In 1982, he returned to coach the team. From 1985 to 1986, he led the Bears to one of their best seasons and their only Super Bowl win.

Halas signed the NFL's first star player. And, he helped get games on the radio.

Ditka was named NFL Coach of the Year in 1985 and 1988.

Star Players

Red Grange HALFBACK (1925, 1929–1934)

Red Grange was a college football star. When he joined the Bears, he became the first major star in the NFL. Thousands of new fans came to see his famous long runs. Grange helped make the NFL more popular.

Bronko Nagurski FULLBACK (1930–1937, 1943)

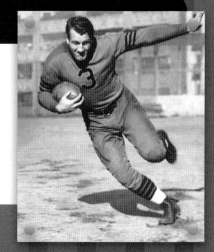

Bronko Nagurski was known for his size and strength. In 1933, he threw two touchdown passes to help the Bears win the league **championship** game. He returned to the Bears in 1943 and helped them become NFL champions again.

Sid Luckman QUARTERBACK (1939–1950)

Sid Luckman led the Bears to four NFL championships. In 1943, he threw seven touchdowns in one game! That was more than anyone in NFL history. It is still tied for the record today.

Dick Butkus LINEBACKER (1965–1973)

The Bears chose Dick Butkus in the first round of the 1965 **draft**. He played for the Bears when the team struggled. But, he was a star. He led the Bears in tackles during his first eight seasons.

Mike Ditka TIGHT END (1961–1966)

Mike Ditka was skilled at blocking and catching passes. This helped change the position of tight end. In 1963, he helped the Bears become the NFL **champions**. In 1988, he became the first tight end in the Pro Football Hall of Fame.

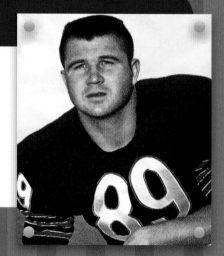

Walter Payton RUNNING BACK (1975–1987)

Walter "Sweetness" Payton led the Bears to their only Super Bowl win in 1986. He was named the NFL's Most Valuable Player in 1977. By the time he **retired**, Payton had set NFL records for most rushing yards and most rushing touchdowns!

Brian Urlacher LINEBACKER (2000–2012)

The Bears **drafted** Brian Urlacher in 2000. He was named the NFL's Defensive **Rookie** of the Year. In 2005, he was named the NFL's Defensive Player of the Year. The next year, he helped the team make it to their second Super Bowl.

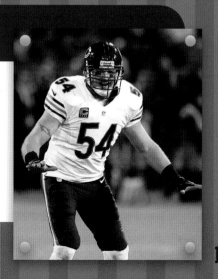

Soldier Field

Home Field Advantage

Soldier Field originally opened in 1924. The Bears started playing their home games there in 1971.

The Bears play home games at Soldier Field in Chicago. It closed for improvements in 2002 and reopened in 2003. It can hold about 61,500 people.

The columns outside Soldier Field are from the original stadium. They were saved when the stadium was rebuilt.

Da Bears

Also Known As

The nickname "the Monsters of the Midway" was borrowed from the University of Chicago's football team long ago. The nickname "Da Bears" came from the television show *Saturday Night Live* in the early 1990s.

Thousands of fans flock to Soldier Field to see the Bears play home games. Some fans call their team "the Monsters of the Midway" or "Da Bears."

When the Bears score, fans sing "Bear Down, Chicago Bears." The team's **mascot** is Staley Da Bear. He helps fans cheer on their team at home games.

Staley Da Bear is named after the team's founder, A.E. Staley.

Final Call

The Bears have a long, rich history. They won many **championships** in the 1930s and 1940s. They became a major force again in the 1980s. They got their only Super Bowl win in 1986.

Even during losing seasons, true fans have stuck with them. Many believe that the Chicago Bears will remain one of the NFL's greatest teams.

Bears fans cheer loudly when their team takes the field!

Through the Years

1921

The Staleys move to Chicago.

1936

The Bears take part in the first NFL **draft**. Their first pick is tackle Joe Stydahar.

1940

The Bears beat the Washington Redskins 73–0 in the league **championship**. No other NFL team has won by that many points.

1920

The Decatur Staleys become one of the first teams in the NFL. Then, it was called the American **Professional** Football Association.

1922

The Staleys change their name to the Chicago Bears.

1963

Red Grange, George Halas, and Bronko Nagurski become original members of the Pro Football Hall of Fame.

1971

The Bears begin playing their home games at Soldier Field.

1984

Walter Payton breaks the NFL's **career** rushing-yards record. His record remains unbeaten until 2002.

2007

The Bears lose in their second Super Bowl.

1967

George Halas coaches the Bears for the last time. He had coached the team off and on for 40 seasons.

1986

The Bears play in their first Super Bowl. They beat the New England Patriots 46–10.

2003

The new Soldier Field stadium opens.

Postgame Recap

1. Who was the coach of the Chicago Bears during their only Super Bowl win?

   A. George Halas   **B**. Dick Butkus   **C**. Mike Ditka

2. What was the original team name of the Chicago Bears?

   A. Chicago Staleys   **B**. Staley Bears   **C**. Decatur Staleys

3. Name 3 of the 27 Bears in the Pro Football Hall of Fame.

4. Why did George Halas choose the team name *Bears*?

   A. Because his nickname was "Papa Bear"
   B. Because the team shared a home stadium with the Chicago Cubs
   C. Because it was his favorite animal

Glossary

career work a person does to earn money for living.

champion the winner of a championship, which is a game, a match, or a race held to find a first-place winner.

draft a system for professional sports teams to choose new players. When a team drafts a player, they choose that player for their team.

mascot something to bring good luck and help cheer on a team.

professional (pruh-FEHSH-nuhl) working for money rather than only for pleasure.

retire to give up one's job.

rookie a first-year player in a professional sport.

Websites

To learn more about the NFL's Greatest Teams, visit **booklinks.abdopublishing.com**. These links are routinely monitored and updated to provide the most current information available.

Index